Jazz, Rags & Blues for Two

4 original duets for early advanced pianists

MARTHA MIER

Jazz, Rags and Blues for Two, Duet Book 5, contains four original duets that reflect the various styles of the jazz idiom. Ragtime, blues and jazz are important contributions to music and are fun to play. Students will love the syncopated rhythms and colorful, rich harmonies found in this collection.

Sharing the "jazz, rags and blues" experience with a duet partner will inspire and motivate students. They will love the challenge of playing these styles that have captured the hearts of performers and listeners alike!

Alfred Music Publishing Co., Inc.
P.O. Box 10003
Van Nuys, CA 91410-0003
alfred.com

ISBN-10: 0-7390-8470-4
ISBN-13: 978-0-7390-8470-0

2

for Angela Kageyama and Sylvia Schroeder

RAMBUNCTIOUS RAG
SECONDO

Martha Mier

for Angela Kageyama and Sylvia Schroeder

RAMBUNCTIOUS RAG
PRIMO

Martha Mier

6

Walkin' Cool

Secondo

Martha Mier

Walkin' Cool

Primo

Martha Mier

Secondo

Primo

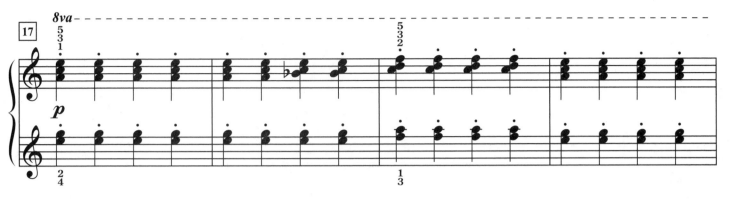

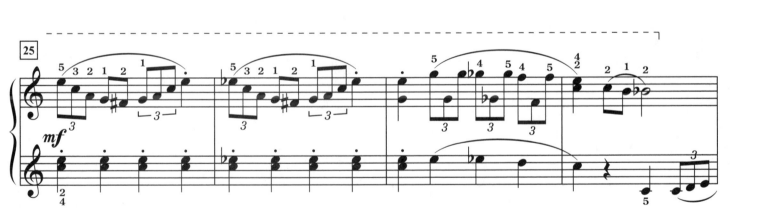

Secondo

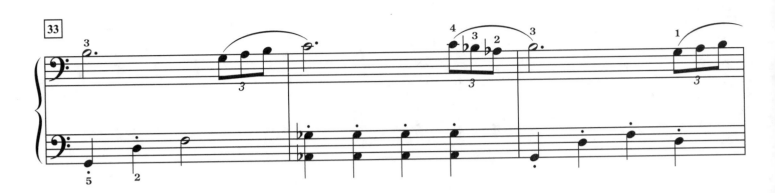

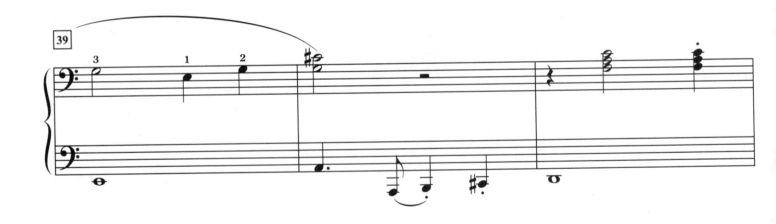

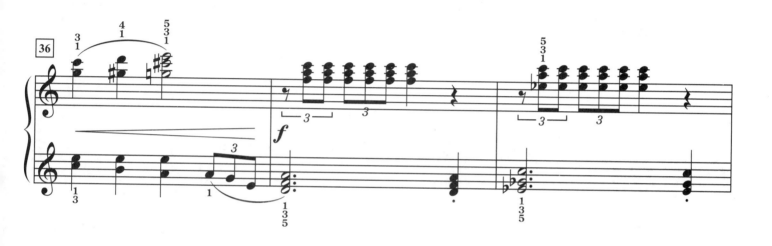

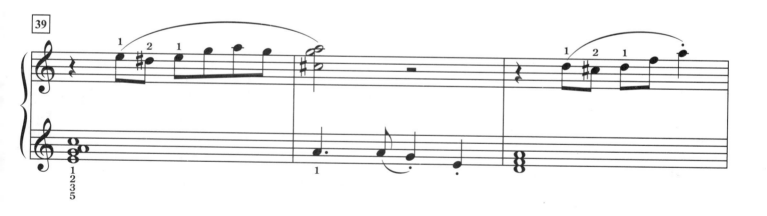

14

Pretentious Jazz

Secondo

Martha Mier

Pretentious Jazz

Primo

Martha Mier

16

Secondo

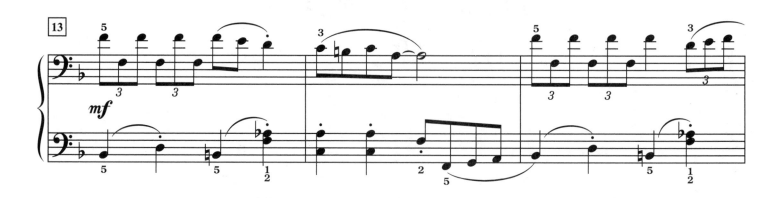

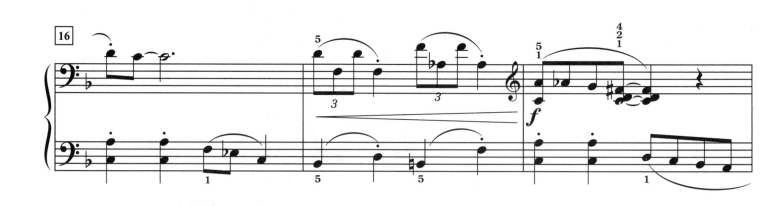

Primo

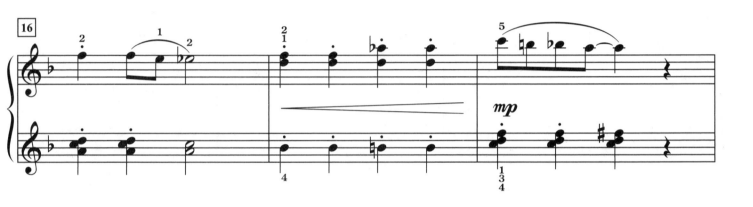

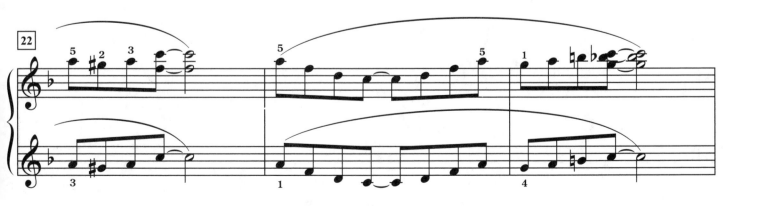

Secondo

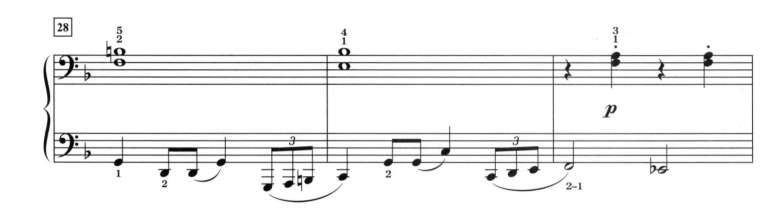

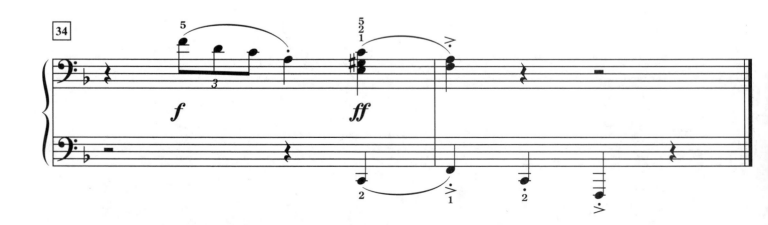

Primo

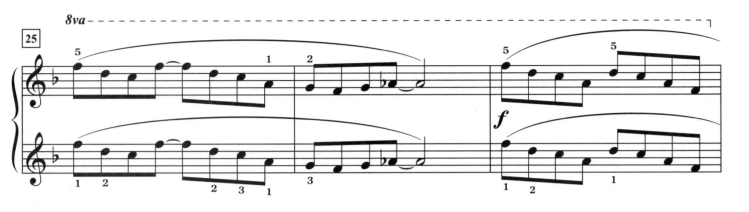

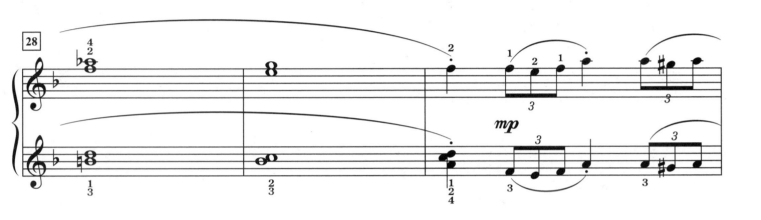

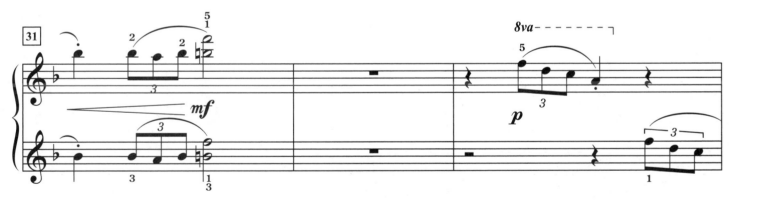

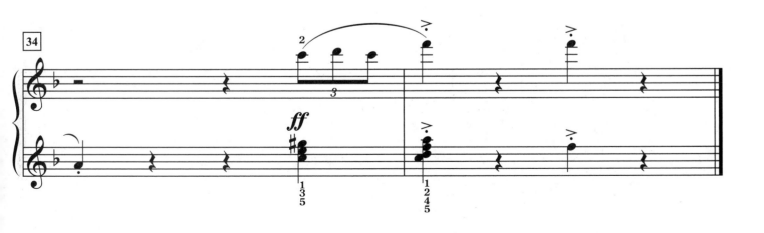

Melancholy Blues
Secondo

Martha Mier

Melancholy Blues
Primo

Martha Mier

Secondo

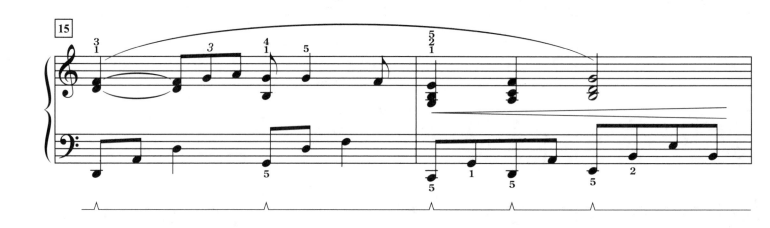

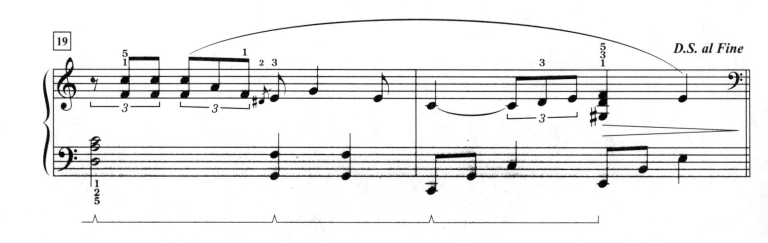

Primo

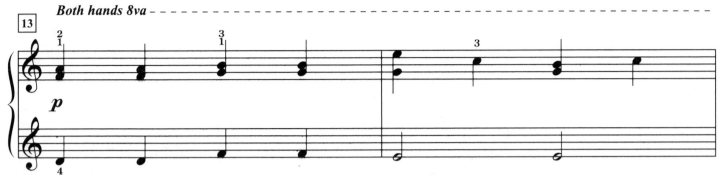

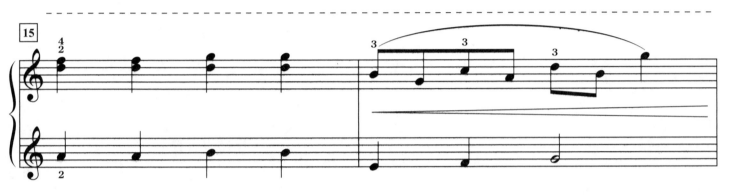

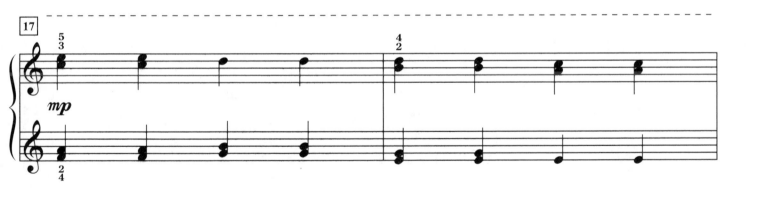

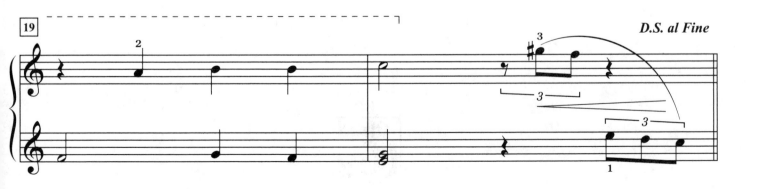